LIBERIA'S
GREATEST FOOTBALL PLAYERS

Where are they now?

"Yes! It is a goal! Jackson Weah scores,"the 32" scores!"

"32! 32! 32!"

Football fans are chanting. It is after 4pm Sunday afternoon again, and ..... The Lone Star players are on the field.

"The Bulldozer!" One fan shouted.

"It was Garrison Sackor, the Bulldozer, who passed the ball to Jackson Weah. Go Lone Star go! Go Lone Star go!" Everyone is shouting with excitement.

The Antonette Tubman Stadium is jam packed with football fans. Ghana Black Star is in Liberia again, playing a friendly match against the Liberian Lone Star.

So many Lone Star fans are now yelling excitedly. "Go Lone Star go! Go Lone Star go! Ghana Black, you will see something today.

En y'all always beating Liberia. Now we're ready for y'all today," a woman chanted.

"Now the score is 2-1 for Liberia! Lone Star is ready for you today, Black Star," another fan replied.

A Little Moment In Travel

This life is a journey we are traveling. Along the way, I must do something for somebody, even if it is bringing out a little smile out of that person. Perhaps striking a conversation, sharing a story or a laughter, if nothing else, then I will be satisfied.

AN OVERVIEW

Our country, Liberia, is a much smaller society, compared to the great United States of America, a multi-complex society way bigger. But there is one very good thing so certain about Liberians. Though we may be living way abroad, way 'behind God's back', we always come together.

We will meet at an association's meeting, where you find all the book people, who will be speaking big, big English, arguing about everything, about anything, even if there should be nothing about which to argue. Then we meet at a party and forget that we were arguing or making palaver the other day, because we love our country. So we put away all our differences and begin to laugh together again. Because why? We realize we have

Jaytoe Anthony Tukan 5

one origin, that's Liberia. We love Liberia. Some of us may not even know the meaning of the word love, nonetheless, we love one another. Some of us, if not all of us, feel there's no better place we could have been born, other than being born in Liberia.

Many of us may establish or re-establish other homes and families way abroad, we still feel there is no better place we will ever call home, other than Liberia. Besides Liberia, there is no better home for us. Liberia is our home. We are Liberians.

The story of football or soccer in Liberia is forever endless. This is a journey, like none other, that we are embarked upon. Sometimes there are obstacles to overcome, bridges to cross along the way. Obstacles and bridges, primarily because this is perhaps the very first time that someone has the audacity to do a story like this. A whole book about Lone Star Players? Has it even been done before? If not, why even bother to try? How far will you go with it? Or how far will the story reach? Some of you may be asking. Trust me, I share your concern.

While I realize the fact that Liberian football players or former football players deserve the honor to talk about them, it is never an easy task to perform. Most of the players whose stories are in this book are living in America. And as such, the busy life in a rapid, fast-paced society like we truly know America to be, the different schedules of former players in different parts of the United States, plus different time zones, all of these become a big factor to consider. With that in mind, I respectfully consider myself an intruder into the lives of these legendary players.

Before moving on, therefore, I want to take this opportunity to express my sincere gratitude for the patience of these very former players for putting up with me, and for not even hanging up and slamming the telephone in my ear every time I call.

Also, I want to pay respect to those former Lone Star players who have departed this life for the life beyond. Additionally, I give thanks to the other former players here with us today, who contributed an insight on behalf of those no longer here.

I am very grateful to you all.

Note: If you are a relative or friend of a former player, who was not mentioned in our story, please know that I did my very best as humanly possible, to reach out to that player. Either I was not successful in getting that legend, or I was

Jaytoe Anthony Tukan

faced with refusal or rejection to include that person's story.

About The Author

Jaytoe Anthony Tukan is the best-selling children's author and novelist of **Kingdom Without A King** and **Playing With Fire.** He holds a Master's Degree in Teaching & Learning with Technology from Ashford University, Clinton, Iowa. He is a Technology Teacher, following a brief career in computer programming.

The last of four children, Jaytoe lived with his older brother, Moses, a newspaper publisher, who took a paper home every day for his younger brother. Jaytoe loved to read some of the articles to his big brother.

Sometimes after reading an article, the lad would be required by Moses to edit and rewrite the article, using his own words, even while the little boy was still in the third grade. This was a task that he didn't like to do. But Jaytoe knew he had no choice in the matter. Eventually, he fell in love with reading and writing. The rest is now history.

For his hobbies: the author loves singing and playing the guitar.

Jaytoe Anthony Tukan

DEDICATION

To my older brother, Moses Chea Tukan, whose love for football and his admiration for these Lone Star Players got me to be very, very interested in football from my early childhood. Moses, you are always the **wind beneath my wings.** I love you, big brother.

Jaytoe Anthony Tukan

ACKNOWLEDGMENTS

I salute Charles 'Babe' Ray Woelfel, John 'Monkey' Brown, Solomon Sipply, Sarkpah 'Rock of Gibraltar' Nyanseor, James Vedier, Teddy Badio, Dominic 'Lucky Shango' Brapoh, Ansumana 'Ansu'[1] Sirleaf. Your willingness and effort to talk about those days that you spent on the football field on most Sundays, has made it possible for a part of the Lone Star Players' story to be a reality in a tangible material. Thank you so much.

Also, I sincerely extend my thanks and appreciation to Mrs. Madea Smith Brown, who was willing to share a light on her marriage to her Late husband, Mr. John 'Monkey' Brown, or Pa Brown, as he was well known in Charlotte, North Carolina.

---

[1]Thanks to 'Ansu' for providing the Lone Star cover photo and other photos for this book.

Jaytoe Anthony Tukan 13

LIBERIA:
THIS SWEET LAND OF
LIBERTY

LIBERIA, Home Sweet Home, there is no place like home. **Oh Liberia,** the gem of west Africa. Oh Lone Star, which shines on every Liberian, and on everyone else within Liberia's borders. **Liberia,** could I have ever been born in a better place? No, **Liberia,** there is no better country on this earth to call my birthplace and my home.

Jaytoe Anthony Tukan

THE DECLARATION OF INDEPENDENCE

THE DECLARATION OF INDEPENDENCE had to pave the way for independence. This was written by Ms. Hilary Teague.Besides the signature of the author of this historic document, eleven other people signed the **Declaration of Independence.**

THE ELEVEN SIGNERS:
Ms. Hilary Teague - Author
John Day
Amos Herring
Anthony William Gardner
Ephrium Titler
Jacob W. Prout
Richard E. Murray
Samuel Benedict
Elijah Johnson
John Lewis
Beverly A. Wilson
J.B. Gripon

Jaytoe Anthony Tukan

This historic document was signed in June, 1847. A month later, Liberia declared herself an independent country on July 26, 1847. **Liberia's Independence Day.**

Jaytoe Anthony Tukan

THE LONE Star: Liberian Flag

THE **LIBERIAN FLAG** is called the **Lone Star**, because it represents the very first African independent Republic. Back then, Africa was still considered a dark continent, and Liberia emerged as the only country to declare herself as a free, democratic, independent nation in Africa. Thus the **Star** in the midst of a blue field (dark Africa) began to shine freely among free world nations as a representative and a voice for Africa. The **Lone Star** has eleven stripes, six red and five white. These stripes represent the eleven signers of the Declaration of Independence for Liberia.

The Liberian Flag was designed in August, 1847, a month after Liberia declared herself an independent nation, making **August 24th** a **National Holiday, Flag Day,** in Liberia.

Seven women designed the **Lone Star, Liberian Flag.** These women were great designers and thinkers, to have envisioned at the time, that the world needed to know that the new Republic of Liberia was in fact a lone representative of Africa, otherwise known as the dark continent of the world in those days.

THE SEVEN DESIGNERS OF THE LONE STAR

Susannah **Lewis - Leader**

Matilda Newport
Rachel Johnson
Mary Hunter
J.B. Runsums
Conilette Teague
Sara Draper

Liberia's Football Legends

TABLE OF CONTENTS

Jaytoe Anthony Tukan

LIBERIA'S FOOTBALL LEGENDS

TABLE OF CONTENTS

Jaytoe Anthony Tukan   21

THE LEGENDS:
THEIR STORY BEGINS

Jaytoe Anthony Tukan

Chapter One
Introduction

The above was a brief background of the birth of Liberia, the Declaration of Independence, and the Liberian Flag, otherwise known as the **Lone Star**. However, there is another **Lone Star**, The Liberian National Football Team. While we will use the word football quite often, we will interchange that word with the word **soccer** at times, to help readers not to confuse it with American football, which is played by a bunch of grown-ups, using their hands (just imagine that).

During my earlier years in America, I asked an American elder, Mr. Robinson, as to while it was called football when players were using their hands to play the game. He said because the ball itself was a foot long; that's why it is called football. So there you have it. Take it or leave it. What else can I tell you?

The Robinsons were a great, caring family. They were good to me. They had two boys in the family. They were from Washington, D.C. It was my pleasure getting to know them.

The former Lone Star Players used their talents, techniques, and skills in creating great legacies that live on even after the players have retired. Today, however, our aspiring young Liberian football players, and even Liberian football fans, know little or nothing about the former players. Their great deeds are also retired with them. Other than a few words of mouth, or some articles here and there, there is hardly any knowledge of many of the players.

I love football. But my elder brother, Moses Chea Tukan, was a big football enthusiast. Sometimes I would watch the Lone Star game with him on the field, or IE and Barrolle game, but for the most part, we both listened to the game on the radio with Henry Andrews' commentary. On behalf of my brother, and for the love of our country, Liberia, and for our high regards for those players, I have decided to pen down some of their deeds in this book.

In doing so, however, it is befitting for me to start with 2004 when the Invincible Eleven (IE) players and the Mighty Barrolle players met in the Queen City of Charlotte, North Carolina, United States of America, in observance and celebration of July 26, 2004. This is when the idea of writing about the former legendary players of the Lone Star truly began. Therefore, the very first part of this book starts in 2004. Please bear in mind that these events will be written and recorded in accordance to how they occurred back in the day (2004).

FROM AMERICA
Liberia's Independence Day - July 26, 2004
Charlotte, North Carolina
United States of America

NEWS LIBERIA

Jaytoe Anthony Tukan   27

Editor-in-Chief

The Editorial

Liberia, a small country on the west coast of Africa, with common boundaries with Sierra Leone and the Ivory Coast, has seen another birthday.

During the weekend of July 26, 2004, Liberia was in the news again. But many Liberians were very proud that this time, the news was different. The war in Liberia has ended! And we hope this time it is for good. We all pray that Liberia will never see war again, that peace will prevail. And peace must truly always prevail.

July is the month that Liberia was born as the first African Republic. July 26, 1847 - 157 years ago (this was in 2004) - Liberia declared herself an Independent Nation. About a month later, the Lone Star, Liberia's National Flag was created

Jaytoe Anthony Tukan   29

by Susannah Lewis, together with six other women.

The Liberian Flag was flown right from that point and was immediately seen over many major buildings in Monrovia, the Capital City, situated in Montserrado County, and then in the rest of the country. While much more can, and should be said about the forefathers, including Joseph Jenkins Roberts, our very first President, those seven women, Ms. Hilary Teague - Author, and the eleven signers of the Declaration of Independence, time may not be gracious for us to do so at this time.

This weekend, nevertheless (July 24, 2004), Liberians came to the Queen City of Charlotte, NC, from different parts of the United States of America, to see the name of the Lone Star being resurrected again. But this time in a different fashion, the Lone Star is the Liberian National

Football Team. Many players of local teams in Liberia back in the day were recruited by the Lone Star. Prominent among those local teams are Invincible Eleven (IE) and the Mighty Barrolle.

The Mighty Barrolle and IE met again on Saturday, July 24, 2004, in observance and celebration of Liberian National Independence Day. They exhibited very well those talents that we had seen over and over in Liberia. *News Liberia From America* also learned several weeks before this weekend that George Opong Weah (this was in 2004)[2], considered to be the world's greatest football player living today, George Sackor and his brother Garrison Sackor, who was famously known as the **Bulldozer** - were all supposed to be here. But they did not come. Though this was not the Lone Star

---

[2]

Team playing on the field, it would have been even more wonderful if many of those legends had shown up. However, fans and players had a great time under such a beautiful weather in the Queen City. The weather could not have been more beautiful, as IE and Barrolle battled it out that day.

1.Reader, please be informed that this story took place when the editor started the production of the news magazine, NEWS LIBERIA FROM AMERICA. The magazine doesn't exist any more, but the editor is thinking about starting it again.

Security Hassle
At Memorial Stadium Entrance
by:
Princess Pwankato
Staff Reporter
&
Young Plato
Contributing Youth Reporter

As we got out of the car, we were surrounded by relatives, as a quick re-union in a way was held. At the gate, some man checked our mother's bag, and a woman said that our dad could not go in with our video camera. So dad was led into another room (possibly a security office) by another man, who by the way, assured our dad that he did not think there would be a problem about carrying the camera in. But he needed the approval of the security supervisor. With the babe in her arms, our mom and the three of us were following daddy. But daddy said we should go ahead and find our seats, and he would join us later. Therefore, the three of us (children) went with our mom.

On the bleachers, I almost fell. Then I heard this woman say, "Ay God."

My mom also said: "Be careful, babe." But I was okay.

Finally, our dad showed up with no camera. After all that bragging the other man did, we were surprised that they did not allow dad to carry the camera in. What is a reporter without a camera? Well, camera or not, a good reporter always has to find a way to get the news.

Therefore, we had to improvise.

The stadium was not as packed as expected. There could be several reasons for this. **News Liberia From America** obtained information from some officials of Barrolle and IE Associations that there was a boycott by some of the Liberians in Charlotte, even some of the prominent members from both teams. Majority of those who went to the game were the Liberian fans from out of town.

The ruling at the stadium was that once you've checked in, you could not check out. If you checked out, you were not allowed to enter the stadium again. We learned later that since the September 11, 2001 terrorist attack, this has been the ruling at all games in the United States. Some fans possibly checked out, but could not check back in. The game was poorly attended.

The game, nevertheless, was well

played. The players were really ready to entertain us. And entertain us they truly did. After the game, our dad interviewed some of the fans. Most of the responses were positive. Only a few fans said that the referees cheated for one of the teams? How could that be? None of the three referees were Liberians; they really belonged to no side at all, as some of us were told, and as far as we could tell. So how could there be any cheating?

Daddy also saw two IE players right outside the stadium and interviewed them. The two players expressed good impression about the game. He wanted to talk to at least two Barrolle players as well. But none of them were available for comments, as people were rushing to exit the stadium.

At the end of dad's interview, one of the IE players said to our mom: "Oh no, lady, are you eating the chicklet, or is the chicklet eating you?" I thought that was funny, to say the least. And that brought a big laughter out of some fans who overheard the comment.

Oh ... I almost forgot. It was good that mommy sent us to look for dad during the game to ask him for some money. We bought pop com, which we enjoyed very much. Overall, I still have a good impression about the game even now. [3]

---

[3]

Princess Pwankato (Saydenu Tukan) was 11 years old in 2004.Young Plato (DavidLee Settro Tukan) was 9 years old. These two children are college graduates today from the University of North Carolina at Charlotte (UNCC). We, the parents, could not have been more proud.

Jaytoe Anthony Tukan 37

What is a reporter without a camera? Well, camera or not, a good reporter always has to find a way to get the news. Therefore, we had to improvise.

Chapter Two

Play-by-Play Action

The game between the Invincible Eleven (IE) and the Mighty Barrolle was played on Saturday, July 24, 2004. This was one of the many programs scheduled in observance and celebration of Liberia's Independence Day, July 26, 2004.

The game was scheduled to start at 4:00 p.m. However, it really did not begin until somewhere around 5:00. The IE players were on the field ahead of time. But the Barrolle players arrived a little late. Nevertheless, fans went to the game to be entertained; entertainment they were going to get.

The two teams matched on the field holding the Liberian Flag. What a great sight it was. Prior to the start of the game, both the Liberian National Anthem (All Hail, Liberia Hail), and the American National Anthem (The Star Spangled Banner) were so beautifully sung by a Liberian lady. **News Liberia From America** was unable to get the singer's name; therefore, her name is not given here. But she sang those two songs very well.

With the IE players in their blue and yellow-strip uniforms, and Barrolle players in their red uniforms, the game then began! First it seemed IE was in control of the ball from the very beginning, but Barrolle continued to take the ball away and began to dominate IE. Honestly, Barrolle was playing IE half-field during the entire first half.

About 15 minutes into the game, an IE

player was given a red card, and therefore ejected out of the game by the umpire. It was surprising to many spectators. Some of us thought that action by the umpire would kill the spirit of the game. But the IE players never wavered at all.

The ruling about a soccer player been ejected is that such a player is never replaced by another player on the team. So there is always an unequal number of players on the football field once a player is ejected. That's exactly the main point of punishments and ejections on the football field. The penalized team suffers.

Mr. Sarkpah Nyanseor, Rock of Gibraltar

Mr. Kalawantis, News Liberia From America International Correspondent, was on the field of play. During the break after the first half, he had the opportunity to interview some of the legendary players of football as we know it. These are former Lone Star players, who were willing to talk about the game. His first conversation was with Sarkpah Nyanseor, also famously known as the Rock of Gibraltar.

Kalawantis: Mr. Rock of Gibraltar, what is your impression about the game so far?

Rock of Gibraltar: The game is good so far; both teams are playing well. But the players on the Barrolle side are more aggressive than the IE players.

Kalawantis: In about the first 15 minutes of play, an IE player was ejected by the umpire. Therefore, IE played the rest of the half with only 10 men against 11 for Barrolle. It seems like Barrolle has dominated the first half. Yet IE is leading by 2 goals to zero. What mistakes are the Barrolle players making?

Rock of Gibraltar: When you have 10 men, you cannot rush. You have got to use the wind (to your advantage). And there are 2 halves in a game; if you rush with only 10 men against 11, you're going to quickly run out of gas. That's why I have decided, along with the other coaches, that we (IE) slow down the game. As for Barrolle, I don't know what formation their coaches told them to carry for which they have not scored yet. They are making simple mistakes near IE goal.

Kalawantis: Could it be due to a solid and strong defense at the goal of IE? What do you think?

Rock of Gibraltar: Yes, that too. Our defense is very strong right now. The guy who is playing #5, I am the one who's coaching him. He is the son of Phillip Clark, one of the best players for the National Team. This fellow is not a defender, just the same way I was not a defender, and I came from the forward line to defense. When you are playing defense, you do not rush; you don't fly all over the field. You've got to delay for others to come (to you). And because of that strong defense, we scored 2 goals. But we will see what happens during the second half, and then I will talk to you again. As I said earlier, every game has two halves. At this point, we do not know how Barrolle is going to perform in the second half. The situation might be different, depending on what happens during the second half. Sometimes football games are unpredictable. You never know until the last whistle blows.

Mr. James Verdier

Kalawantis: Mr. Verdier, From the very beginning, an IE player was thrown out of the game, so IE was playing with 10 men against 11. Yet IE has 2 goals to zero at the end of the half. What is going on here? What mistakes are the Barrolle players making?

Mr. Verdier: Our boys are doing very well, but they are making simple mistakes. As soon as they correct those simple mistakes, the game will get back in our favor.

Kalawantis: There were so many ejections today on both sides. What is your comment on any type of ejection today on the Barrolle side?

Mr. Verdier: I believe all the ejections on

both sides were fair and necessary. The guy who was ejected on the Barrolle side at the end of the first half realized he was the last man (in his area); so he felt he had to play a foul like that against the IE player. That's why he got put out. That's one reason why IE is ahead right now.

Kalawantis: And now it is going to be 10 against 10 during the second half because a Barrolle player was also ejected. Do you think Barrolle needs to change its formation? By the way, I thought Barrolle dominated the first half of play.

Mr. Verdier: It is so true Barrolle dominated the first half. But Barrolle's defense has to re-adjust. The guy that's in the Barrolle goal is not a real goalkeeper. Barrolle's goalkeeper is coming in a few minutes. Once the real goalkeeper gets into the goal, and Barrolle re-adjusts like that, the game will be in our favor. Barrolle still has the chance of winning this match.

Mr. Charles 'Babe Ray' Woelfel

Kalawantis: Early in the game, an IE player was ejected, and IE played with only 10 men against 11. Yet, IE is leading by 2 goals to zero. What is your impression?

Babe Ray: Right now, this is a very tough game. I had played the game for Liberia for many, many, many years, and I know that anybody can win the game at this point. So far IE is in the lead by 2 to zero. But this does not mean that Barrolle can not beat IE. Barrolle can come back in the second half and score 2 goals. I played against IE before; IE was leading three goals before, and in less than the last fifteen minutes of the game, we were able to redeem and win the game. So I know that Mighty Barrolle can do it again.

Kalawantis: Now a Barrolle player was also thrown out at the end of the half. What does Barrolle need to do in the second half, now that it is going to be 10 against 10?

Babe Ray: Well, they are down now by 2 goals. What they need to do is to score 2 goals, and (then) put in another one. To do this, they have to tighten up their defense, especially the mid-field. In the middle, they are very, very weak. They need to tighten up their defense and make sure that they score.

After the end of the game, **News Liberia From America** again spoke to Mr. Charles 'Babe Ray'Woelfel, who patiently agreed to speak to us for the second time.

Kalawantis: Mr. Babe Ray, You said

during the break that Barrolle could actually come from behind and win this game. Even though they did not win, but Barrolle tied the game. They really dominated and played the second half very, very well.

Babe Ray: Well - being a veteran player for the Mighty Barrolle, I knew that we could do it. Looking at the game, Barrolle was still the better team. During the second half, IE mid-field became useless, to say the least, and Barrolle was able to take advantage of that opportunity. So we were able to tie the game.

Kalawantis: Some of the IE fans said that the referee cheated IE by throwing their players off the field until IE played with only 8 men against 10? What do you think? I mean, it doesn't seem fair.

Babe Ray: Well, that's the rule; the referee was following the rule. If a play commits a foul, he should be penalized. Our players were also penalized. I didn't see any cheating in that.

Kalawantis: From the great performance of the Barrolle players in the second half, it seemed they were going to win, except for the fact that there was no more time left in the game. Any thoughts?

Babe Ray: That's exactly what I was telling you during the break. If we had at least five more minutes in the game, Barrolle would have won. Our boys were the better team even during the second half.

Chapter Three

FOOTBALL CONVERSATIONS
WITH MY BIG BROTHER

When elder brother Moses took me
away from our parents in Maryland
County, the northeastern part of Liberia,
all the way to Monrovia, the Liberian
Capital, Montserrado County, that was
the era of Liberia's Greatest Football
Players, like Jackson Weah, Garrison
Sackor, his brother George Sackor,
Wannie Botoe, Josiah Johnson, John
'Monkey' Brown, Charles 'Babe Ray'
Woelfel, David Momo, to name but a few.
As someone coming from Gbarken,

Forpoh, a little interior village so far away from Monrovia, I had never heard of these guys in my life. Moses would lecture me about some of them.

My dear brother, Moses, the man who is the **wind beneath my wings,** was himself a sports lover and a football enthusiast. As humanly possible as I can, I will recreate some of the conversations between the big brother and me, about the Liberian Football Players.

When he was in his football mood and excited about those legendary players, most especially when those guys were on the field of play at the time, Moses' lecture to me and some of my friends, would want to make us, and it sometimes actually made us, to start running to the Antoinette Tubman Stadium.

Some of my friends and I would really go to the games without the proper fee, which was, for the most part, only ten

($0.10) U.S. cents for children. We would jump the fence to get into the stadium to see those players. Who were those guys and where did they come from? What made them to stand out like that? Where did they really learn how to play football? Those were some of the questions I would ask the big brother, especially when he and I were alone.

Sometimes Moses would answer some of those many questions. "Most of them learn how to play the game right here in Monrovia. Jackson Weah is a Kru boy from New Krutown. He also has family people here in Clara Town (where we lived). Garrison and his brother George are from Maryland County; I think they are Grebo boys," my big brother would say.

"We are from Maryland County, too. That makes us Grebo boys, Right?" I would ask my big brother. As a little boy who was very much unknown, maybe that was my way of seeking some kind of connection to some famous people.

Moses would smile and say, "Yes, we are Grebo boys, too, little brother."

"But I heard that George and Garrison play on two different teams. Garrison plays for IE, and George plays for Barrolle. If they are brothers, why do they play against each other? It seems like they do not like each other. Why?"

I would inquire of my big brother. I could not see or understand how I could ever play against my own brother, just in case he and I were football players. Could anyone blame me? I was just a little boy who did not understand that rivalry did not mean that the two people are enemies. This was just a game.

My big brother would simply smile. "No, little brother, Garrison and George are brothers. They like each other; in fact,

I believe they love each other. Garrison likes IE, and George likes the Mighty Barrolle. They are not enemies at all," Moses would tell me.

"Who is the older brother? Is it Garrison or George?" I asked the big brother, like it did matter so much. What has this to do with the game, right?

"George is older than Garrison," Moses said.

"But what about Marr Sarr? His name sounds different and funny. Where is he from?" I asked my big brother.

"Well, I am not very sure. I think they say he's from Gambia. Now let us get back to listening to Henry Andrews," the big brother would say, somehow running out of patience with me. After all, we were listening to the game. Many of those questions could always be asked and answered anytime, even when the game is not on.

Well, on this note, my brother gets himself to blame here. After all, I was minding my own business in the village. Then he took me from there - away from our parents, away from our two sisters, away from my friends, carrying me all the way to a place called Monrovia, to send me to school. Then instead of sending me to school right away (I did not go to school the first year Moses took me to Monrovia), he is teaching me the 3rd grade at home. Why? **'We were catching hard time'**. Additionally, he was lecturing me about football players, some of whom I may never be able to meet. So big bro, don't you get tired with me asking questions about these guys.

Of course I could never voice out those words to my big brother (just thinking them within my heart). Are you kidding me? At no time should you dare talk to your big brother like that, most especially, when he's trying to make your life better for a brighter future.

Here is one thing Moses did that I did not like, but I never complained about it. He put me among those Monrovia boys to sell newspapers from the office where he was working as a publisher. I did not even know good English, and this man is doing this to me? I was always afraid of those boys, especially when we all met at our gathering place at 12 noon, the Treasury Department on Broad Street. The purpose of the gathering was to compare notes, to see how best we could help motivate one another. Was there a boy who did not finish selling his papers at the time? How best could the other boys help him in gaining more customers. You should now know that I was always the kid behind everyone else in meeting deadlines. This idea of being a newspaper boy, though I did not like it, helped me a lot. I learned English fast, from those fast, English speaking Monrovia boys.

Moses, after completing junior, at the Bafu Bay Mission School in Greenville, Sinoe County, decided to relocate himself to Monrovia. Moses told me later that the mission was owned and operated by the Baptist church. Those very nice Baptist Missionaries did a great job educating him and other Liberian children. But most importantly, those good missionaries introduced him and the other children to Jesus Christ.

By the time Moses took me to Monrovia, however, he was already with the Assembly of God Church on Buchanan Street, Monrovia. Later on, Moses would also introduce me to some Assembly of God Missionaries, some of whom I would later live with. Others I worked for - selling the Bibles and other books on the sidewalk, from the Christian Literature Book store.

Then my life took a different turn, in a good way, for the most part.

But Our parents, Jacob Jlateh Tukan and Mary Gbarlee Tukan, including the three of us, the other siblings, Bessie, Ida, and I, we were all expecting him back home in Maryland County. The whole of Gbarken Town was expecting Moses for a big celebration for his graduation. He was the first child from the town who completed junior high school, which was the equivalence of today's high school graduation. But there you have it, dear reader. Moses never went back home. He decided to move himself to a city called Monrovia. Just imagine that, so far away from all of us.

When I talk about being away from

family and friends, dear reader, do not even think I was angry about Moses taking me away from our village. On the contrary, I was excited.

In my village, the highest level of education at the time that some of my friends could get was the 2nd grade. I had just completed the 2nd grade when my brother took me away, because he knew what was ahead. All the children in my village started school late, because teachers were not available during those days. I was still living on the farm when the Catholic Church sent Teacher Sackor Freeman to our village. My friends started school when I was still a farm boy, wasting time, until a year later.

I was around eight years old when Bessie's husband, Paul, registered me in the kindergarten session of Forpoh Public School. Therefore, some of my friends were around 14-16 years old when they completed the 2nd grade. Most of them, with no other school around beyond the 2nd grade level, got married and settled down. Moses did not want that for me.

It was probably around 8pm when our bus from Maryland County reached Monrovia, perhaps after about seven days on the road. You might ask, 'that long?'

You see, we stopped and spent two or three days in Zwedru, Grand Gedeh County, where Moses and this Forpoh girl fell in love right after meeting each other for the first time. It was perhaps 'love at first sight.' In my hearing when we were boarding the bus to take off for Monrovia, Moses promised to send for that girl. However, that never happened. I wonder what went wrong between those two love birds. Oh, well, I guess life went on fine for that beautiful girl without Moses. Elizabeth was beautiful!

We are now headed to Clara Town

where my brother lived. Those great street lights were brightly shining. I had never in my entire life seen a city so bright and well lighted at night, like it was broad day. Still on the bus, I turned to my big brother and asked, "So this is Monrovia?"

Moses looked at me - with a glow of joy on my face, and answered, "Yes, little brother, this is Monrovia."

I wanted to be sure. So I asked him again. "This is where you've been living all these years?" I didn't even know how long Moses had lived in Monrovia before going home to get me.

My brother sensed something was up - that something else was on my mind, beyond just that question. He hesitated a little. After some pause, he said, "Yes, my little brother, this is where I have been living. This is where you will be living from now on."

Truly, I was about to get vexed with him - that he had been living in Monrovia all this time, enjoying life, and I was still in the village? But I was too little for our parents to let me go anywhere, anyway. At the time Moses took me away was the right time for me to leave the village.

I was not vexed at all; the glow on my face became even brighter. The idea that I was going to be living with my big brother in Monrovia? Then, to Moses' relief, I think I hugged and thanked him, the best way I knew how. I can not even put in words how excited and happy I was that night. If we were living in America at the time, perhaps I would have said to my brother, 'I love you.' But we Liberians (Africans in general), are not raised in Africa to do crazy stuff like that.

Okay now, enough about me. We've

got to get back to the main story at hand. We have to continue the story of the Liberian football or soccer legends. After all, this book is about them.

In addition to Moses lecturing me, sometimes listening to Mr. G. Henry Andrews, who is the greatest sports commentator and entertainer to me, always added more kerosene or gasoline to a raging fire inside of me, for the need of wanting to be on the football field, at the Antoinette Tubman Stadium. With Henry Andrews' radio commentary, you always had to grab those sneakers or slippers (in my case) from the closet or from under the bed and get going. I may miss the first half of the game. But I always knew I would be there while the second half was underway.

I always struggled, or had a hard time

(from the Liberian way of speaking) getting through the gate. Maybe I only had five ($0.05) cents, which was never enough. Well, I could still get through the gate, because someone at the gate would accept what I had. After all, it was the second half, and the game would soon be ending. So why can't you let a child in?

En five cents that money? Who tell you say five cents that not money (Liberian colloquial)?

So I was always in. What a sweet Liberia in those days. Those great glory years some of us might not see again, but I hope Liberia will get somewhere close someday - to those glory days.

En five cents that money? Who tell you say five cents that not money (Liberian colloquial)?

Jaytoe Anthony Tukan

Chapter Four

PLAYERS OF THE
1960S & 1970S

Jackson Weah
John 'Monkey' Brown

Jackson Weah
The Lone Star Center Forward

Jackson Weah was known for his '32 Style' (Jackie Style) he played in every game, or almost every game, to score a goal. For me and so many Liberians, we have always believed Jackson Weah invented the '32 Style.' Till this day, nowhere else in football history have I ever seen or heard that someone else could play this style better than Jackson.

He was a small-body man, probably 5'7" tall, who played center forward, usually wearing jersey number 9 for the Lone Star. This position in football is the goal scorer. I mean, others can score, when the opportunity arises on the field, but the main individual in this position is the go-to-player first.

Moses explained. "When Jackson was right in front of the opponents' goal, he always demanded that the ball be sent to him above ground, at least above his waste or above his shoulders. While he is in that position, ready to score, do not ever send the ball on the ground to Jackson Weah. He will almost always immediately send it back to you."

"But why? He did not know how to play or control the ball on the ground? He only knew how to play the ball in the air?" I asked my big brother.

Laughing, Moses said, "Learning how to play starts from the ground. All the players who play for the Lone Star National Team truly know how to control the ball on the ground, for them to get to be put on the team for the whole nation."

"Oh...okay," I said.

"If the ball was sent to him properly (as his back is turned to the goal), he would then flip himself over and kick the ball into the goal. It was so difficult for any goalkeeper to catch such a ball because of the brilliant way Jackson Weah played that style. I have no knowledge about any other football player truly coming out with such a style of playing," my big brother said.

In addition to my brother and I believing that the '32 Style' was Jackson Weah's invention, I asked two legends: 'Monkey' Brown and 'Babe Ray' about this during the July 26, 2004 festivities in Charlotte, North Carolina, USA.

John "Monkey" Brown said, "I never saw any other player to play the style so well. It was Weah who invented the '32

Style.' He was the only one who could play it very, very well."

"Is this particular style legal today in football?" I asked the legend.

"As far as I know, this style is still legal today. But these days, I only watch a football game once in awhile. And every time I watch, I do not see any other player playing the '32 Style' any more. But it is still legal," 'Monkey Brown said.

"But even if someone did, do you think that person would play the style any better than Jackson Weah did?" I asked the legend.

Pa Brown indicated, "Even when I played the game against Jackson, or on the same side with him, some players would attempt to play the style. But nobody ever played the '32 Style' any better than Jackson Weah did. He was the inventor. Only he could play the '32 Style' the best."

'Babe Ray' also agreed that the '32 Style' is still very legal today. "Even in our days when Jackson and I played the game, there was no other player who could play the style any better. And I don't think there is any player out there today who can do that. He was the inventor. Who else could play the '32 Style' as good as the inventor himself?" the legend said.

During the 2022 World Cup, I even watched some of the players actually attempting the 'Jackie Style', as a former Lone Star Player, Solomon Sipply, calls it. But nobody played that '32 Style' as good as Jackson Weah was described by his fellow legends to be the best player of the 'Jackie Style'.

Mine! Mine! Mine! Jackson Weah was a **True Legend.**

The author has no knowledge, where Jackson Weah might truly be today. Or whether or not, he is still alive.

John 'Monkey' Brown is one of the  greatest Liberian football players, perhaps the best Lone Star defender ever to play the game. Passing by him was never an easy task to accomplish by any opponent. To get to David Momo, perhaps the best goalkeeper ever in his days for the Lone Star, you had to first pass by 'Monkey Brown. Some players found it very impossible to pass by John 'Monkey' Brown.

He was born John Brown on October 15, 1940, unto the union of Thomas and Jennie Brown, right in Monrovia. But somehow as he got to be a popular football player, the name John Brown disappeared from the radii. So if you wanted somebody to know whom you were talking about, you've got to say, John 'Monkey' Brown or simply say, 'Monkey' Brown. This new way of calling the legend originated from his colleagues on the football or soccer field. Therefore, for almost his entire life, his colleagues on the field, his fans, and football spectators, only recognized the man as, 'Monkey' Brown.

Because of his brilliant way of playing, in addition to his leadership skills on the field, it is said that 'Monkey' Brown was promoted or picked (drafted) by the

Mighty Barrolle, which was a senior team to JET, a junior local club with which he was a player.

The Liberian Lone Star is comprised of so many great players, drafted from local clubs or football teams. Some of the local teams are: The St. Joseph's Warriors, JET, Bameh, Mighty Barrolle, the Invincible Eleven (IE), Kotoko of Logan Town, the Survivals of Clara Town, LPRC Oilers, to name but a few.

He was perhaps the greatest Fullback (the main defender in front of the goal) ever to play for the Liberian Lone Star. He wore jersey number 5. 'Monkey' Brown played the longest time in the history of football in Liberia. His playing years date as far back as 1954, when he was about fourteen years old. He was one of the original football players of the Lone Star, right after the initial formation of the national team by John Howard around 1963-1964. So John 'Monkey' Brown played from that time until his retirement from the game in 1976. Pa Brown, as he was affectionately known in Charlotte, North Carolina, was a St. Patrick's High School product in Monrovia, completing in 1960.

During the playing eras of players like 'Monkey' Brown, 'Babe Ray', Jackson Weah, Garrison Sackor, George Sackor, Josiah Johnson, these individuals only played for the love of the game, as Liberia did not have any appropriated budget to pay those players. The love for the game and the love for country – was the reason why they played, and nothing else.

Like many of the players, who would travel abroad after retiring from football,

'Monkey' Brown traveled to the United States of America with his first wife, Famatta, originally settling in Atlanta, Georgia. He and Famatta Brown were married for 34 years. From their beautiful, long-lasting and loving union, were born four children. They are: Josephine Brown, Alocious Brown, Comfort Brown, and Oretha Brown.

After living in Atlanta for many years, John's loving wife and lifetime partner, Famatta Brown, passed away. Eventually, John 'Monkey' Brown relocated to Charlotte, North Carolina, to begin his next chapter.

In the year 2004, I sat with Pa Brown at his Charlotte, NC residence, and had a conversation with him. "As popular a football player as you were, and with so many women throwing themselves at celebrities like you, what made your marriage to Famatta last so long?"

He replied, "Not just loving each other, but also understanding each other and working through your problems. Believe me, every marriage has problems. We understood each other very well."

"I believe you still have good memories about your playing era. Of all the players on the Lone Star Team, name at least one player, besides you, whom you admired very much," I asked the legend.

Pa Brown answered, "Garrison Sackor is that player who stands out."

"Why Garrison?" I followed up.

"For his dominance on the field. He really bulldozed his opponents, especially in the goal area, and he did that so well and very brilliantly," the former Fullback told me. That's why he got that title.

"Was Wannie Botoe the best dribbler Liberia has ever seen?" I asked Pa Brown.

The legendary Fullback said "Yes, Botoe was the best - the best I had ever seen, and the best dribbler I ever played football with."

"Is there anyone who comes close to Botoe today (2004)?" I asked him again.

'Monkey' Brown truly, emphatically said, "Nobody comes close to Botoe as far as dribbling, ball control, and techniques. To me, he will always be the best dribbler."

"Why do your fellow players and fans consider you the best fullback or the best defender ever - for the Lone Star?" I asked the legend.

Pa Brown smiled and said, "Perhaps because of two things that stand out about me. I am a no-nonsense defender, and a penalty specialist."

With that answer, the legendary football player brought the laughter out of me, as he and I started laughing. We laughed so long and loud, almost like we could not control ourselves.

As our conversation was coming to a close, I had the audacity to ask Pa Brown the most unthinkable question of the whole dialogue, going to the Fullback position again. Actually, I was putting the legend on the spot - to hear what he would say about himself.

"Was the 'Monkey' the best Fullback in his days, or ever - for Liberia?"

The legendary player decided to ask me his own question."Why do you continue to go back to this fullback thing over and over?"

"It is because this time, I want to hear from you, not what the people say, but what do you say about yourself?"

Pa Brown laughed and then said, "My man, you're trying to test me, to get me in trouble?"

I answered, "No sir, I am not trying to get you in trouble. But if you don't want to answer this question, to speak for yourself, about yourself, it is okay. I can leave the question alone, and not bother you any more."

'Monkey' Brown said, "Well, I do not want you to feel like I don't appreciate you wanting to write about me and my fellow football players. After all, I haven't seen anything that someone else wrote about us. So, I will answer the question.

What was the question again?"

"So you want to tell me that you forgot the question already? Well, I will ask the question again?"

"Yes, ask the question again. I want to get the answer right when I give it to you," the legend said, laughing again.

"Okay, here we go. Was John 'Monkey' Brown the best Fullback in his days, or ever for Liberia?"

"If you were to take a vote, most likely, everyone would say I am. But times change and situations also change every day. There are so many new, young Liberian football players out there. Honestly, I do not watch football games very often these days," the legend said.

With that answer, I felt the legend did not want to seem like he was bragging about himself. He tried to be modest. For the time I had known him in Charlotte, he was always that honorable, humble, respectful guy. I didn't want to push him any longer, because there was no way I could make him to change from his modesty and talk about himself.

Even for Michael Jordan, whom most basketball fans, including me, consider to be the best basketball player ever, never one day said that he was the best player. Michael would sometimes ask the person who is asking him that question. "If Bill Russell won more champions than I did, you tell me who is the best in basketball?"

But I felt that perhaps Pa Brown had more to say on the Fullback position. Maybe there was someone else on his mind who could be as good, or almost as good as he was, if not better than he was. So I followed up with another question for the Fullback position again. "Who do you think comes close to you today?" I asked him.

Pa Brown answered, "I believe it is the fellow called, Washington Blade. He is a very good and tough defender."

Then I asked the legend if whether or not, he had some advice to our young and aspiring Liberian football players today.

John 'Monkey' Brown indicated, "I would advise everyone: put your mind on the game. I know in my days, we played for the love of the game. These days, some players get paid. But regardless, just put your mind on the game, and nothing else."

On March 29, 2003, Pa Brown got married to his second wife, Madea Smith. Madea Brown was not home when I interviewed her husband in 2004.

So in 2018, she was kind enough to allow me into her home. I had the opportunity to sit and talk to her about their great union.

"Who was John and where did you two meet?" I asked Mrs. Madea Smith-Brown, John's beautiful wife.

She replied, "John was a quiet, very easy-going man. He did not talk much. Sometimes I had to get words out of him."

"I know you and Pa Brown got married in 2003. How did you feel marrying to a famous, former football player, one of the greatest players Liberia has ever produced?"

"First of all, I am not so much into sports. I did not meet him when he was playing," Mrs. Madea Brown emphatically said to me.

"So how did your meeting come about? Did someone introduce the two of you to each other?" I asked.

"When he moved to Charlotte, one of his friends gave him my number. And one day, I received a phone call, and it was John 'Monkey' Brown. I was surprised. That's how we met. We met right here in Charlotte, North Carolina. I did not know him when he was in Atlanta, Georgia," Mrs. Brown replied.

"So how would you describe your marriage to John 'Monkey' Brown?" I asked again.

"Our marriage was good. As I said, John was an easy-going man. So what could ever go wrong in our house?" Mrs. Madea Smith Brown indicated.

I laughed and said, 'what could ever

go wrong in our house' enee[4]?
After five years and eight months of a great marriage, Madea's loving, easy-going husband, John 'Monkey' Brown, passed away in Charlotte, on November 25, 2008. Madea Smith-Brown still lives in Charlotte, North Carolina.

4

'Thanks to Mrs. Madea Brown for providing 'Monkey Brown's picture in this story.

Chapter Five

PLAYERS OF THE
1960S & 1970S

Charles 'Babe Ray' Woelfel
Solomon Nyonpeh Sipply

Let me use this opportunity to acknowledge the fact that after he departed Charlotte, North Carolina, at the conclusion of the July 2004 Independence Day festivities, 'Babe Ray' did not return 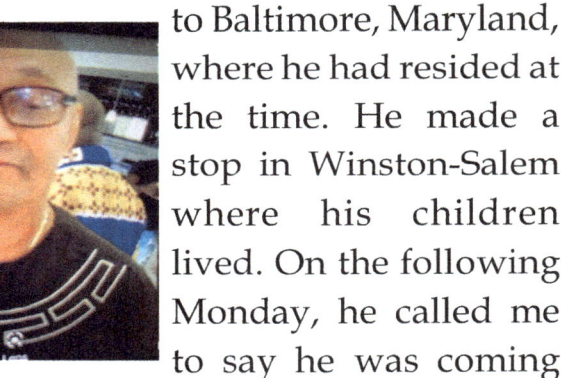 to Baltimore, Maryland, where he had resided at the time. He made a stop in Winston-Salem where his children lived. On the following Monday, he called me to say he was coming back to Charlotte to sit with me and continue the Lone Star story. Boy! Was I very, very excited and humbled to welcome him to our home. He really spent that whole afternoon with Veronica and me, giving us valuable information, which you will see later in this story. I truly appreciate what the legend did.

So this legendary player, Charles 'Babe Ray' Woelfel, who was originally coming from Mighty Barrolle, was drafted as a mid-fielder to the Liberian National Team around 1963-1964. Wearing jersey number 4, he played a total of twelve years. Being a great veteran of the game, 'Babe Ray' is very knowledgeable about the Lone Star and its founding years. He and 'Monkey' Brown gave me a great background history from the birth of the Lone Star. Both of them indicated that the Lone Star Team came into existence around 1963-1964.

"I know that the team was called the Liberia National Team, starting as far back as 1952, until somewhere around the mid-1960s....say around 1963-1964, when it became the Lone Star Team," 'Babe Ray' indicated.

I asked the legend the same question as put forth to every other former player. "I believe you still have good memories about your playing era. Of all the players on the Lone Star Team, name at least one player, besides you, whom you admired very, very much."

He replied without hesitation, "The player who stands out the most to me is Wannie Botoe."

Then I followed up, "I have heard so much from my big brother and other people about Wannie Botoe. So, Why does he stand out so much to you?"

'Babe Ray' replied, "Botoe was a very, very different player. This young man could dribble the whole field, like there was nothing to it. He did that brilliantly."

"So was Wannie Botoe the best

dribbler Liberia has ever seen?" I asked.

'Babe Ray' replied "Yes, Botoe was truly the best to me."

"Is there any other Liberian football player in the past or today (2004), who comes close to Wannie Botoe?"

To this question, the legendary player answered with no hesitation again, that "There is no other player close to Botoe in dribbling and ball control. I mean, this fellow was very, very different. He had techniques, tactics, and skills in football that nobody else had."

"I know some labels were attached to certain players by the way they played the game. For example, John Brown was called John 'Monkey' Brown. Why was Sarkpah Nyanseor called the 'Rock of Gibraltar?'' I asked.

"Sarkpah was a very, very tough defender at the goal. He played a very hard defense, like 'Monkey' Brown did. Therefore, that title was assigned to him by G. Henry Andrews, a great sports commentator," he told me.

"What about Garrison Sackor, whom they called the bulldozer? My big brother talked about this fellow so much, like he was a superhuman. How did that label or title come about?"I asked the legend.

"That was exactly how he played the game. It was because of the way Garrison bulldozed his opponents," he replied.

"Speaking about titles or labels, why is Charles Woelfel called 'Babe Ray?'" This time I put the legend on the spot.

'Babe' means 'petty' (as in small), rouge (red - in French), or yellow man, because of my skin color. It seemed like I was also the smallest, or looked like the smallest player on the field. Petty rouge," "Babe Ray' said.

'Babe Ray' loves the game of football. He has a very good, retentive memory of his playing days, and knows great facts and information about football. He still remembers his very first international game when the Lone Star played against the Black Star of Ghana in 1964. He had just joined the team. The game ended in a score of 1 goal to zero in favor of the Black Star, according to 'Babe Ray.'

'Babe Ray' is the first Lone Star player to have occupied the position of president for his local team, the Mighty Barrolle.

After graduation from St. Patrick's High School in 1964, 'Babe Ray' enrolled at the university of Liberia to study forestry. He graduated in 1968, and matriculated about two years later (1970) to Yale University in the United States of America. He graduated in 1972 with a master's degree in Forestry. As of the writing of this story, Charles Woelfel is the only Lone Star player whom I know, to have obtained a doctorate degree. He earned a Doctor of Philosophy Degree, (Ph.D),1993, as an Environmental Science & Forestry major. He is a great educator.

Where is Charles 'Babe Ray' Woelfel today? 'Babe Ray' resides with his wife in Winston-Salem, NC, after he retired as a school teacher from the Baltimore public school system. He and Marion Woelfel have been married for more than fifty (50) years. Out of their great union were born four children. They are: Charlene Woelfel, Kamah Woelfel, Marchelle Woelfel, and Christopher Woelfel.

I asked the legend, "How would you describe your wife and your marriage?"

He replied, "Marion is a great lady and an excellent wife. I have an excellent marriage. I couldn't have asked God for a better partner."

I followed up, "Being a veteran player of the game of soccer or football back in the day, with all the popularity that comes along, not to even mention the so many, many women from everywhere, throwing themselves at you, how has your marriage survived, for you two to be together all these many, many wonderful years?"

He answered, "Understanding, my young man. Marion and I understand and trust each other very well. That is an important aspect of any marriage."

Speaking about Marion Woelfel, the author of this book, actually worked with her at Chase Manhattan Bank, Monrovia, Liberia. Those years we spent at the bank were some of the good old days that some of us still remember and talk about today. Hopefully, Liberia will gain ground again very soon.

So speaking to Marion, I asked, "Do you still remember Anthony Tukan?"

She replied, "How can I forget you? We worked together at Chase. And I think you were the Chase Manhattan News Editor there."

Going back to the long-lasting union of the couple, I asked Marion. "Babe Ray being the celebrity that he is, what makes your marriage to be long-lasting, like you two have been married forever?"

She laughed and said, "We are friends. It starts with love, but love alone is never enough. Understanding and trusting each other is very important. We understand each other. We trust each other."

"So how difficult or easy was it, for you to be dating somebody like 'Babe Ray', the popular football player, back in the day?"

"First of all, I was living across the bridge and minding my own business. He was the one coming to my place and pursuing me. When I saw the seriousness in him, I had to ignore whatever else, even though he was telling me he had fifty-three (53) girlfriends."

"Really? He was telling you that he had fifty-three girlfriends when the two of you were dating? And you still went ahead and married him?" I asked Marion.

She laughed again and said, "Even today, he still tells people that he has fifty-three girlfriends. I can't mind all that."

Marion brought the laughter out of me here, as we both laughed. I remarked,

"Wow! 'Babe Ray' still tells people he has 53 girlfriends today....hahaha!"

Solomon Nyonpeh Sipply was another great soccer player, wearing either jersey number 2 or 5. He was drafted by the Lone Star in 1972. He was also appointed the team captain, and played for the Lone Star until he retired in 1979.

Like 'Babe Ray', Solomon is a player who also remembers great facts about his playing years. He still has good memories of the 1979 6-Nation Tournament. He took part in that great tournament, and had a great experience, especially that year being his very last, playing football.

I asked the legend the same question I put to everyone in the Lone Star story. "I believe you still have good memories about your playing era. Of all the players on the Lone Star team, name at least one player, besides you, whom you admired very much."

He replied, "That player will always be Waka Heron."

I followed up, "Why Waka?"

Solomon replied, "Waka was a great player, who never quit playing until the last whistle of the game."

Solomon Sipply, like Pa Brown and 'Babe' Ray, indicated that Jackson Weah was the inventor of the '32' Style he used to play. He said, "We also called that style 'Jackie Style' back in the day. And today that style is known as the Bicycle Style."

"In your view and as much as you can remember, was David Momo the best goalkeeper of Liberia in his days?" I asked the legend.

"Not only was he the best goalkeeper at that time, but David Momo was the best in Africa as a whole," the former team captain replied.

Solomon is the product of Monrovia College Industrial Training School, graduating in 1971. The following year, he enrolled at the University of Liberia, and attended from 1972-1973. He later matriculated to the State University of New York in Morrisville, where he obtained his Associate's Degree.

Solomon Sipply has five children. They are: Phillip Sipply, Koffa Sipply, Tanyennoh Sipply, Nyonteh Sipply, and Nateena Sipply.

Where is Solomon Nyonpeh Sipply today? This former Lone Star player lives in Minneapolis, Minnesota, United States of America, with his beautiful wife, Danlette Benson Sipply.

Chapter Six

LAST PLAYERS OF THE 1960s & 1970s

Garrison Sackor
Wannie Botoe

Garrison Sackor: The Bulldozer

According to my elder brother, Garrison Sackor was affectionately known as the Bulldozer, because he was always very, very dominate at the opponents' goal, when his team was awarded a corner kick. Like Jackson, Garrison often played forward. But unlike Jackson, who was a small-body individual, Garrison, on the other hand, was a huge fellow, probably between 5'9"- 6'5" tall. At no time was he ever the kicker of the corner kick.

Garrison, however, would stand directly in front of the goalkeeper when the ball was kicked to him from the corner. My big brother said, "While the ball is in the air - coming towards the goal, Garrison would step on the

Jaytoe Anthony Tukan

goalkeeper's foot to prevent him from jumping up for the ball. So by the time the ball came down, it was Garrison, the goalkeeper, and the ball: all three would be in the net. It is a goal! This is why everyone calls him the Bulldozer. He truly bulldozed his opponents around without mercy, even including the goalkeeper."

"That type of playing sounds like a foul. But the referee does not blow against him?" I asked my big brother.

"This style of playing happened in a flash that even the three referees were confused. There should have always been a whistle blown against Garrison for stepping on the goalkeeper's foot. But there was never a whistle because nobody ever saw what happened, or how it happened. It happened so fast!" Moses said.

As you might have already read in this book, I spoke to 'Monkey' Brown and 'Babe Ray' about Garrison. These two veterans of football gave me their descriptions of the 'Bulldozer.' They both agreed Garrison got that label or title because of the way he played the game.

'Monkey' Brown said, "He bulldozed his opponents, especially in the goal area."

'Babe Ray' added, "That was exactly how he played the game. It was because of the way Garrison bulldozed his opponents."

The author has heard that George and his little brother, Garrison, were in America. But there is no sufficient information whether or not they are still here, or if they are alive.

Wannie Botoe
The Best Dribbler Of His Days

Wannie Botoe, also known as Wanibo Toe, was very different and distinct from the above players. For the purpose of this writing, we are going to stick with the name Wannie Botoe. I believe Botoe was very, very, very different from every other football player in the history of Liberia's football. During his days, he was known as the best dribbler on the football field. Even today, there is still the speculation or the debate that Wannie Botoe was the world's best dribbler during his days. It is said that only one other individual, Stanley Matthews, a player from Great Britain, could be compared to Botoe.

Speaking of comparison, I watched a short video of Sir Stanley Matthews playing football and dribbling everybody. He was very, very good. So, I understand why people would talk about him whenever they have a conversation about Wannie Botoe in those days. I tried also to find a video of Botoe playing football. But I was not successful.

Honestly, I never saw Wannie Botoe play. I was very young. But I can always relive the games through the eyes of my brother, whose narrating abilities were very superb. In fact, besides our dear mother, Mary Bawion Gbarlie Tukan, and my school teacher, Augustine Sir Gborie from Bong Mine Elementary School at Zaweata in Bong Mines, Bomi Hills, Liberia, the only other person who always stands out in storytelling is my brother. He is the best narrator/storyteller I have ever known.

"While it is the aim of every player to score and help to win the game, Wannie Botoe on the other hand, never concerned himself so much about scoring. He was the player who would set-up the plays for others to score," Moses said.

"So he never scored a goal at all, even when his team was having trouble scoring?" I asked my big brother.

"Yes, he sometimes scored, when he knew his team was struggling. But from the spectators' point of view, however, scoring was not his major concern. Botoe could dribble the whole field. Sometimes while faking the goalkeeper, he would walk straight into the goal, and then pick up the ball and carry it to the center of the field. That was one of the few times he actually wanted to score, and one of the few times that he scored," Moses said.

"Yes, that's another thing I never can understand. Why would he or any other player really pick up the ball from the opponents' goal after scoring?" I asked the big brother.

"It was that player's way of saying, yes, just see what I can do to your team; you can not touch me. You can not ever stop me. It is like bragging or bluffing the other side without really saying a word," Moses said.

"But that action could make the other team start a fight. Right?" I asked the big brother.

"Yes, it could, but nobody ever started a fight because of that."

You know, with a patient brother like Moses was, I always had more questions to ask him. "So what were the players on the other team doing? They were just standing around and let Botoe dribble and walk into their goal like that?"

"His opponents were not standing around. They were playing and some of them were falling down all over the field because of the way Botoe was dancing around and faking the ball to them. Little brother, let me just tell you another thing Botoe used to do."

"What was that?" I asked my big brother, with the anxiety or what you might call, the eagerness within me. I could not wait to hear what else he had to say about Wannie Botoe.

"Botoe would sometimes dribble the whole field, and reaching in front of the goalkeeper, then refusing to score, and would begin to dribble all over again. Who could ever stop a player like that? Wannie Botoe did not only play football, but he entertained the spectators very, very well."

In front of the goalkeeper and refusing to score? I knew at this point that my big brother might have been exaggerating a little bit about Wannie Botoe. But it didn't matter that much, because I was always truly enjoying Moses entertaining me about these great players, some of whom I had never seen or met.

A slim-body man, probably more than six feet tall, it is said that Wannie Botoe was born unto Liberian parents in Ghana. He grew up in that country. He learned how to play soccer there, and became a teammate of a local team, perhaps the Republicans, one of the Ghanaian soccer clubs. I am told that while he was in Ghana, the Black Star, the Ghanaian National Team, almost always beat the

Lone Star. That alone would make someone like me to think that Wannie Botoe played for the Black Star. I could not get any confirmation on this. I did a research, but the result lead me nowhere.

Some former Lone Star players say Wannie Botoe was on the Ghana Black Star Team. Other players dispute that claim. Nevertheless, when Botoe finally went back to his home country, and joined the Lone Star, it then became very difficult for Ghana to defeat Liberia again.

Wow! What a **Legend.** What a **Legend!**

Wannie Botoe passed away in Monrovia in 1967. Even though I was very, very young at the time, I was one of the many, many viewers at the Sports Commission on Broad Street who actually viewed the body of the Legend.

THE ONLY PLAYER OF THE 1970S & 1980S

 Sarkpah Nyanseor, famously known also as the 'Rock of Gibraltar' is the only player in our story, with the playing era from the 1970s to the 1980s. He was also a great player for the Lone Star Team.

Wells-Hairston High School has truly and truly produced great individuals who became a contributing part to the Lone Star. Sarkpah was one of the graduates in 1978.

Jaytoe Anthony Tukan

Sarkpah matriculated to the Indiana Technology University in Fort Wayne, Indiana, United States of America. There he began his Associate's degree study in Technology.

Originally from River Cess, Sarkpah was born on September 26, 1956 in Monrovia, Liberia.

Sarkpah started playing football or soccer, as some people call the game today, with the Majestic Football Team, possibly a junior team to IE, before joining the Invincible Eleven. First, he was playing in the left-out position with IE, wearing jersey number 11 in 1973. Then in 1974, he was recruited by the Lone Star, playing in the same position. After sometime, it seemed the Lone Star could not use him in that position, so he left and went back to IE. Instead of putting him in the same position,

Sarkpah's coach switched him to defense, wearing jersey number 5.

That prompted me to ask my very first question of the legend. "Why did the coach switch your position?"

"I think he saw that the team needed somebody in defense. The IE coach saw something different in me that nobody else saw, not even myself."

"But it seems like there was a roller-coaster between IE and the Lone Star concerning you. So how did you end up playing for the Lone Star again?" I asked the 'Rock'.

"When the Lone Star saw me playing a tough defense on the IE team, they decided to carry me back for the defense position."

"Speaking about playing the defense, I listened to many radio commentaries with my father. In my hearing, I often heard Henry Andrews, best commentator to me, referring to somebody as the 'Rock of Gibraltar.' Was that you?"

"Yes, I was the one that Henry Andrews always called the "Rock of Gibraltar."

"So, as far as you know, there was nobody else referred to as the 'Rock'?"

"As far as I know, there was nobody else during my playing years. However, you can ask other former players and hear what they say about the label or title. 'Monkey' Brown played a very tough defense before my time. So it is possible that he might have been given that title as well. Other players could have been given that label before I started playing for the National Team," Sarkpah said.

"So it seems to me that the title came about from your tough defensive playing. Is that right?"

"Yes, that's correct. That's why I was saying to you that John 'Monkey' Brown could have been assigned that same title before my time. He was a very tough defensive player, also wearing jersey number 5," Sarkpah said.

Switching gear, I asked the legend. "I believe you still have great memories about your playing era. Of all the players on the Lone Star Team, name at least one player, besides you, whom you admired very much?"

"That player is Benedick Wisseh," Sarkpah said.

"Why Benedick standout to you?" I decided to follow-up.

"Benedick had a lot of skills in ball control on the field. He will definitely be the one that stands out to me."

Sarkpah played for the Lone Star from 1974-1983. Even though he left and traveled to America, he was always called back home to play during major games, like the All Africa Cup, or the West Africa Cup. When the Black Star, the Ghanian National Team, had to play the Lone Star, he was always there and ready to represent his country.

So, the idea that a player, who has left the Lone Star and is now abroad, would return to Liberia and play on the Lone Star Team again, actually confirms the statement of Brucien Myers, a former official of the Liberia Football Association (LFA). He said that the players do not ever leave their local teams. Even though they are put on the National Team or are playing abroad, they are still on their local teams (like St. Joseph's Warriors, Jet, IE or Barrolle). They can go back or be recalled anytime to play on that team.

=========================

The trophy you see in this story was awarded to Sarkpah by his American soccer team, Heimes, from New York, for being the Best Defender during the 1985-1986 Season. It goes without saying that our dear 'Rock of Gibraltar', truly continued to play professional soccer during his earlier years in America. Though Benedict Wisseh could not be reached for his story in this book, Sarkpah unselfishly told us that his Liberian teammate, Benedict, also received an award for being the Most Valuable Player (MVP) for the 1985-1986 Season for the same team, Heimes.

Where is the 'Rock' today? Sarkpah Nyanseor lives in Providence, Rhode Island, with his beautiful wife, Ankie Morris Nyanseor. The couple has four children, three girls and one boy.

I asked Sarkpah, "What makes a good and strong marriage?"

"A good and strong marriage comes about when the couple, not only loves each other, but also loves and cares for other people. My wife loves and cares for other people. That makes a big difference in our marriage," the legend told me.

Mrs. Ankie Nyanseor, the daughter of Barromy Morris and Nancy Peters, is a Register Nurse (RN).

"I think he saw that the team needed somebody in defense. The IE coach saw something different in me that nobody else saw, not even myself."

Jaytoe Anthony Tukan

Chapter Seven
PLAYERS OF THE
1980s & 1990s

Following the era of great Liberian football players like those just described above, came another era for other great Liberian football stars, some of whom were my classmates. Raymond Godfrey and Paul Broh were my classmates in the 8th grade at the C.H. Dewey Junior School, in Bomi Hills, Liberia. Anthony Gray (famously known as AGray, the Teacher) was also my classmate in the 9th grade at St. Patrick's High School in Monrovia. I think he was called the Teacher by the fans because of the way he played. When the ball was in his possession, and using his fingers, he would direct his teammates to where he wanted them to position themselves. Wherever he pointed his finger, a teammate better be there, because that was where AGray would send the ball.

Raymond Godfrey, who was also my classmate in the 8th grade, actually became a visiting coach on the weekends to the Chase Manhattan Employees' Football Team, of which I was a teammate.

Godfrey was a disciplinarian, who did not care so much about whether you were a friend or a former classmate. He would treat you the same way he treated other players. But for some reason, I thought I could take advantage of the former classmate relationship.

We were always supposed to show up on the field, somewhere around the Sinkor Airfield area, at about 6:45 every Saturday morning. You were never consider late until after 7:00. Workout time was 7:00-7:30am. The first mistake I truly made was showing up at 7:10am, when my teammates were already working out. He gave me a verbal warning, indicating that he was truly everybody's coach, and would definitely treat all players the same way, regardless of past relationship.

You would think I should have paid heed to that first warning and friendly advice. Two or three Saturdays later, I went late again, but this time, for fifteen minutes, at 7:15am. Do you want to know something? Godfrey ordered me to do 25 pushups, or I would not be allowed to play on the team any more. He was not even a Chase Manhattan employee; but I was. He was just a volunteer coach. Can you imagine that? But I had to comply.

That was Raymond Godfrey, alright. He was the disciplinarian I came to know on the football field.

Did Raymond Godfrey play for the Lone Star? I heard from a few former players that he did. Other former players said that he never played tor the National Team. I was not in Liberia at the time during the 1980s or 1990s. So I can not definitely say yes or no to that question. So, this is your question to answer, dear reader. Did Raymond Godfrey ever play for the Liberian Lone Star?

Originally, Godfrey played for the St. Joseph's Warriors.

Players of the 1980s & 1990s

George Opong Weah
Teddy Phillip Badio

George Opong Weah

The years 1990s were facing out. Or to put it plainly, the 1990s were ending. The Year2000 or the famous Y2K was about to arrive, when I found myself among the many employees of IBM, also known as the International Business Machines Corporation, in Charlotte, NC. It was towards the end of 1998 when IBM hired me to be a computer programmer. During my high school years, IBM was a company of my dream. I had always wanted to grow up and work for good-old IBM someday. Even when I started interacting with the employees of IBM, who were coming in and out to transact business at the Chase Manhattan Bank where I worked, in Monrovia, Liberia, I was all the more motivated to work for IBM. You probably can tell at this point how happy I was, being an IBMer. I was very, very excited, to say the least.

So I found myself among fellow computer programmers, many of whom were mostly Americans. They started a conversation quite different from what we had to do at work.

You live in the United States, but Opong lives in France, so far away from you. Both you and Opong are from the same country. But you, yourself, have not met the famous football player in real life. Nonetheless, your co-workers know you are originally from Liberia, and so they begin to chat with you about George Opong Weah.

"Do you know that the greatest football player living today comes from Liberia?" Some of them would ask you. Actually, they are about to lecture you about Opong.

"No kidding, I never heard of him," you jokingly answered their question. Now if these were Liberians you were talking to, they would have known that you were just kidding when you said you've never heard of Opong. But since these guys are all Americans who really do not relate to how Liberians talk, they take you seriously. Still not getting the fact that, as Americans, if they have already heard about this football player, obviously, they should know that you, a Liberian who loves football, must already know about him.

"You've never heard of George Opong Weah? Are you from Liberia for real?" At this point, your American co-workers are now challenging your nationality.

They have a great point here, because if you do not know about Opong Weah, and you claim that you are a Liberian who loves football very much, you are probably not a Liberian. Or, you may be a Liberian, but living on another planet, not Planet Earth – for you not to have heard about George Opong Weah.

So, you realize Americans are too slow when it comes to understanding the way Liberians talk. Forgive their ignorance and just tell them in plain American English what they really want to know.

Finally, you tell the truth and nothing but the truth. Yes, you do know about Opong much more than they do. Some of them, now relieved that you really live on Planet Earth, are happy to tell you what they heard or know about the player.

"Every country in the world wants him. Especially countries in Europe, they will pay any amount to have him play on their team. He lives in France, or is it Germany?" Some of them are not sure, but speculating about the player.

But you enjoy the conversation, the praises for the player, anyway. Why? Because this is your country boy these people are talking about.

"He gives money to so many charitable organizations; he also gives money to many poor children in the world," they excitedly explain to you.

Because you are also from Liberia, you have a feeling of pride and dignity. You feel connected to the player. As you hear these praises of a Liberian and of Liberia, your face begins to glow, you actually begin to blush. After all, everybody is talking about your country because of your country boy, George Opong Weah.

Then the question you were most likely trying to avoid is what one of them asks you directly. "Have you met Opong yet?"

Everyone now turns to your desk, to hear what you would say. If you say yes, you better be sure it is the truth, because you will then be bombarded with all the questions many of them are ready to drill on you. Questions like When? Where? How? Did you talk to him, or play a football game with him? So you better say no, if you have not really met the player.

But your answer is No, and you think okay now -- case closed. Let's get back to work. No more questions. Palaver finish ooo (a Liberian way of speaking). Right?

Jaytoe Anthony Tukan   137

But you are wrong; you better think again. One of them calls your attention again and says, "But wait a minute, Jaytoe, don't you want to meet him?"

"Surely, I would like to meet him. But where? Do you want me to go looking for him around the world? I may know where he lives, but where he is at this moment, I do not know. So what do you suggest I do?" You finally ask these guys your own questions.

"Well, I guess you have a point there." Your American coworker, who seems a little perplexed, answers your question.

Now he may be thinking that you do not appreciate the fact that this is your country boy they are praising; this is your country, Liberia, which is the center of attention in a good way for once in perhaps the last 20 years (2004). Contrary to what this American might be thinking, you are very proud of Opong; you are very proud of Liberia.

========================

Then one day, you receive a call from a friend, Patricia, telling you she hears that George Opong Weah, the Greatest Football Player in the world today (2004), is coming to your city.

"Did you hear that Opong is coming to our city?" Patricia asks.

You don't believe her. "You better get out of town, Patricia! You know Opong is not coming here," you say.

But she insists that what she has heard may really be true. "I think Opong is coming to our city," she says.

"Okay, Patricia, let me call you back in a few minutes. I will have to call a few other friends around town," you say.

"Okay, please do; because if Opong is

really in our city, I truly want to meet him," Patricia pleads with you.

Then you call another friend; that friend calls another friend, and the word spreads around. They all tell you that the player is already in town - in a city called Charlotte, North Carolina, where you live, United States of America.

You know that this is a once-in-a life time opportunity. You've got to find a way to meet this player, perhaps play on the same side with him, or play against him. Or, maybe, if nothing else, play one-on-one against him.

So you now call your friend back. "Hey, Patricia, you were right. Opong is truly in Charlotte. I will get the details and tell you later where you could possibly meet him."

She is happy and says, "Okay, Jaytoe, I will be waiting for your call. Please do not forget about me, Jaytoe. I am serious"

"Okay, Patricia, I will call you back as soon as I find out. Even if you don't meet him personally, I can get his autograph for you," you jokingly tell Patricia.

"Jaytoe, you already said you will let me know where I can meet Opong. Please do not tell me about no autograph." Patricia takes your words seriously.

"Patricia, Patricia, I was just kidding with you. Be patient. As soon as I find him, I will call you," so you put her mind at ease.

The date was March 20, 2004. That was when I met Opong! It was on the football field on Shamrock Drive, near Eastway Drive. The guys were already working out with the Super Star when I arrived. Since I hadn't met the player before this date, I could not recognize him from the rest of the players who were all working out. I knew some of the players, but not all. I asked a fellow standing on the sideline of the field. "Which of those guys is Opong?"

He replied, "You don't know George Opong Weah?"

"What kinda question is that, man? If I did, would I be asking you?" I asked the fellow again.

"Oh, you really don't know him. That's Opong in the green t-shirt," he finally believed me.

I thanked the fellow and walked over to Opong and introduced myself. Shaking hands with him, I said, "Opong, I am Jaytoe. It is very good to meet you."

I wanted to say more - say something like I have always looked forward to this day. But he did not give me the chance. Perhaps I would not have finished even if he did not cut me off. I may have been a little nervous. Okay! Okay! So I was a little nervous. It is not like you get to meet a guy like that every other day in your lifetime. So even if I was shaky or nervous, could you even blame me?

He replied, "It is good to see you, too. Now get to work," He invited me to join the workout. After all, I was already in my football clothes. What else was I going to do there? So we worked out! And we worked out!! And we worked out!!!

Then we played a friendly game, with Opong and I on the same side (of course not by my own choosing). We had team captains who did the selections.

About fifteen minutes into the game, I remember very well how I was in the right position to score, and Opong was supposed to pass the ball to me. First he looked at me, and it seemed like he was about to pass the ball to me. Instead, Opong changed his mind, but decided to score, though he was not in the right position to score. He missed the goal. It was a great miss.

Later, he confessed, "All I had to do was to pass the ball to you because you were right there in front of the goal. Instead, I became very selfish with the ball and I missed."

"Yes, I was standing right there and waiting for the ball," I replied.

"I am sorry about that, my man. We still have a game to play; right?" the Superstar, George Opong Weah, really apologized to me?

"Yes, we do. There is more game to play," I said.

Oh, I almost forgot to tell you about Patricia. Yes, I called her during the end of the first half. It just happened she lived about twenty minutes from the Shamrock Field. Patricia arrived when the second half was in progress. At the end of the game, I introduced Patricia to Opong. She shook hands with the legend. Patricia truly received Opong's autograph. She was very excited.

As to who won the game that day, please do not ask me that question, because it is one thing I could not tell you. I forgot. After all, it was just a friendly game. Nobody received a trophy.

Where is George Opong Weah today? As we speak, Opong lives in Liberia. He is the President of Liberia.

Teddy Phillip Badio

Teddy Phillip Badio is another great Lone Star player. Wearing jersey number 4, he played defense for four years, from 1982-1985.

I asked Phillip the same question I ask every other legend, "I believe you still have good memories about your playing era. Of all the players on the Lone Star team, name at least one player, besides you, whom you admired very much."

Phillip replied, "There were some great players I played with on the team. But the one who stands out the most is Anthony Gray (AGray).

"Why AGray?" I asked Plillip.

Phillip replied, "AGray was a very

good player; I mean, he was a great player whose skills and techniques were amazing. He was truly a motivator. It was always amazing being on the field with him."

"Who are some Liberia's football legends, though you never played during their era, but they stand out to you?" I asked Teddy.

"Even though I never played during the playing years of the 1960s and the 1970s, two people stand out to me. John 'Monkey' Brown was the best defender. David Momo was the best goalkeeper of Liberia in those days."

"What would be your advice to young and aspiring Liberian football players today?" I asked.

Phillip replied, "Play from your heart, not for money."

Phillip Badio, like Sarkpah Nyanseor,

is a graduate of the Wells-Hairston High School in Monrovia, Liberia. He has five children. They are: Teddy, Jr., Asia, Anna, Marie, and Terrance.

Where is Phillip Badio today? Phillip lives with his beautiful wife, Musu Badio, in Charlotte, North Carolina, United States of America. The couple tied their knot on October 23, 2003.

Chapter Eight

PLAYERS OF THE
1980s & 1990s

Dominic 'Lucky Shango' Brapoh
Ansumana 'Ansu' Sirleaf

Dominic Jaryenneh Brapoh, otherwise known as the famous 'Lucky Shango', became a teammate of the Lone Star in 1985. Wearing jersey number 9, he played center forward for the team. As I have mentioned in this book  before, a center forward is truly that go-to player as far as scoring. Honestly, any other player who has the opportunity or in the right position at the right time, in front of, or not too far from the opponents' goal to score, can kick the ball into the goal. But the center-forward is the player who has the most ample

Jaytoe Anthony Tukan

chances to scoring.

Dominic Brapoh had actually played for Kotoko of Logan Town and a few other local teams, before joining the Mighty Barrolle. Then he joined the Lone Star and played for a period of three years, from 1985-1987 before retiring.

I asked Dominic the same question I have asked every other player: "I believe you still have good memories about your playing era. Of all the players on the Lone Star team, name at least one player, besides you, whom you admired very much."

He said, "George Opong Weah without a doubt was that player who always stands out in my mind."

"Why Opong?" I asked Dominic.

"His practicing was not different from his game. Whether we were practicing or playing an actual game, he was always serious the same way. He would never stop playing until the last whistle of the game or practice. That's what made him to stand out like that."

"After their retirement from the game, hardly do we hear about so many Liberian football players. What they are doing, where they live, whether still in Liberia or abroad, people do not know that much about these legends. But this situation does not apply to you. It seems you are even more popular now as a singer than you were as a football player. How did you end of singing?"

Lucky Shango answered, "Music was my first passion before football. I was always singing, but nobody knew me at the time."

Lucky Shango's most popular album is Beautiful Woman, which was released in the year 2003.

I asked Dominic, "How did the label or title 'Lucky Shango' come about? Did you acquire it as your stage name for being a singer?"

He replied, "No, that label came from the football field, and I carried it with me as a singer."

"Really?" I was surprised to hear that. So I followed up, "Many of your fans, including this humble admirer here, always thought this was your stage name from music. So how did that come about on the football field?"

He replied, "Many of my teammates started calling me like that because of the many lucky chances I had in scoring a goal. Quite often it was always amazing to them that I seemed to be right there when one of my colleagues would pass the ball to me and I would score, like it was a lucky chance."

Jaytoe Anthony Tukan   153

"But you were the center-forward. Isn't that the major duty of a center-forward, the go-to player to score?"

"Yes, that is true. However, any other player can still score a goal, and some of my teammates scored goals, too. But for some reason, they seemed to be always surprised or amazed about the way I used to score," 'Lucky Shango' said.

Dominic added that his teammates took the name from 'Lord Shango', portrayed by some famous tribal chief or king (perhaps from Africa) in a movie.

Dominic attended Brooklyn College in New York, majoring in Liberal Arts. Here are his children: Slewion, Tarlor, Nahju, Kalihqua, Mahilda, Baygboe, and Dominic, Jr.

Where is Dominic Jaryenneh Brapoh

today? 'Lucky Shango'[5] and his beautiful wife, Nikki Gibson Brapoh, are living in Atlanta, Georgia, USA

5

1. According to a brief research by the author, Dominic is correct that his teammates took the title from 'Lord Shango.' It is also a 1975 movie. I have not watched the movie. Don't we learn something every day?

Ansumana & Naomi Gbaa Sirleaf

Every now and then, I hear someone say, always remember where you come from. Or someone else may say, how can you know where you are going, when you don't even remember, or you may pretend that you don't remember, where you come from? Not remembering where he comes from is not applicable to this

Liberian Football legend, 'Ansu'.

'Ansu' was another great Lone Star player. This legend joined the team in 1989, playing for seven years until his retirement in 1995.

He was a very good defender at the goal line, wearing either jersey number 2 or number 3. This is the right-half-back, or left-half-back position, and it all depends on which number a player is wearing that day.

Not only does 'Ansu' remember where he comes from, he also still talks about those good-old days, including many of those friends with whom he played the game of football or soccer.

"Which team did you play for - before joining the Liberian Lone Star?" I asked 'Ansu'.

He replied, "It was not just one team. I played for so many teams. Here are some of them: Mayanabo of New Kru Town, Stewart United Brothers of Gardnersville, the Powerful Eagles of Gardnersville, Fulani FC of Central Monrovia, LPRC Oilers of Gardnersville, and Kotoko of Logan Town."

"Wow! Of all the Lone Star players I have been talking to, your playing era 'takes the cake'. You must have had so many friends, playing for so many teams like that," I said.

'Ansu' laughed and said, "Yes, I had so many great friends from every team. Some of them are: Dominic 'Lucky Shango' Brapoh, Sam Chebli, Charles Banabas, Nathan Naplah, Augustus Julu, the Late Alfred Kullen and the Late Blama Kamara."

I asked Ansu the same question that I have asked every other Liberian football legend: "I believe you still have good memories about your playing era. Of all the players on the Lone Star team, name at least one player, besides you, whom you admired very much."

He said, "George Opong Weah, without a doubt was that player who always stands out in my mind."

"Why Opong?" I asked 'Ansu'.

"Opong Weah was an inspirational player. Because of his brilliant, driven skills, he made playing the game look very easy to do, like there was nothing to it. I really enjoyed playing during his time," 'Ansu' indicated.

'Ansu' was born in Claratown, Monrovia, Liberia, unto the union of the Late Alhaji Soko Abrahim Sirleaf and Haja Sando Kaidii Sirleaf. The names of Ansu's children are: Bendu Mentu Sirleaf, Soko Abrahim Sirleaf, Sabrina Ansuma

Sirleaf, Jumah Amily Sirleaf, Angie Sirleaf, David Christopher Greene, and Naosu Destiny Sirleaf.

'Ansu' graduated from Monrovia College Industrial Training School in 1984. He matriculated to the University of Liberia where he studied Business Management & Economics. Like some of our players travel abroad after retiring from the football field, 'Ansu' traveled to the United States of America.

Then I asked 'Ansu', "What really makes a good marriage?"

'Ansu' said, "A good marriage comes about when the couple truly understands each other and keeps their commitment to each other."

Where is Ansumana today? 'Ansu' lives in Philadephia, Pennsylvania, with his beautiful wife, Naomi Gbaa Sirleaf and their children.

Chapter Nine

The Complexities & Wonders of Life

When God created life, He made sure to include creativity in all human beings. Life, as we know it, is full of complexities and wonders. While some of these may be negative, like the sorrows we face, our low moments in time, there are also wonders in life that we, human beings actually create, or wonders that may be the good act of God, which can not be explained. In any case, we enjoy.

We pay money at the movie theaters to see our favorite movie stars. Sometimes it is not necessarily that our favorite actor or actress is in that movie. Our interest or desire to see the movie may be because of what we hear about the movie, so we take the time to carry our family to see the movie. For some of us, it is time for relaxation, time for getting away from the pressure life has to offer outside of that.

But do we ever, even wonder how that movie was made? Who are these people behind the scenes, those who are behind all such creativity?

'Why should it matter to us, as long as we pay our money. Right?'

If you might be thinking of asking me that question, you are right. We should not even care about all that stuff. Human brains do create; human beings pay and enjoy. That is part of the creative wonders of life.

Equally so, we see, admire, and worship our Liberian football players. Well, in all reality, when I say worship, I am using this word lightly, not from the literary sense, because it is only God whom we should worship. Nevertheless, we hold these guys, the football or soccer players, in high esteem, in very high admiration for their creative, God-given talents. So, some of us talk about them like they were superman.

Behind the scene, however, there is the Liberia Football Association (LFA), which is the force behind all that talent. We could not bring this book to an end without sharing a little information about the Liberia Football Association.

The LFA was founded in 1936. While we could not confirm the true founder,

Mr. John Howard, who is the Founder of the Lone Star, is considered to be the Father of the Liberia Football Association. This is the organization which actually has authority over all football sports activities in the country.

Twenty-six years into its existence, the Liberia Football Association became an affiliated member of the Africa Football Union (WAFU) in 1962. It was the same year (1962) that the LFA also gained an affiliation with the Confederation of African Football (CAF). Additionally, The LFA joined the membership of the world's highest ranking and official football organization, FIFA, in 1964.

In this book, we previously expressed how difficult it was for us to find some former Liberian Lone Star players in America to speak to us. However, we did not anticipate that it would be even harder to speak to some officials of the Liberia Football Association in Liberia.

While we were able, through a research, conducted by Mr. Kalawantis, our dynamic, energetic International Correspondent at **News Liberia from America,** to obtain the names of the current officials of the Liberia Football Association, we were faced with much more difficulty to speak to any of them directly. We learned that the current officials are: Mr. Mustapha Ishola Raji, President; Mr. Sekou Konneh, Vice President; Mr. Isaac Montgomery, General Secretary; Mr. Jallah Corvah, Treasurer. This was the information we obtained from the website of the LFA. However, none of this was confirmed, because efforts by Mr. Kalawantis to interview some of these officials were in vain.

Additional research, nonetheless, has revealed a former official of the Liberia Football Association, in the person of Mr. Brucien Myers (living in America today), who agreed to briefly talk to us. Mr. Myers was once a member of the Executive Committee (EC) of the Liberia Football Association. While he was on the Executive Committe, Mr. Myers also served as the President of the Inter-Schools Sports Association (ISSA).

INTERVIEW WITH AN EC MEMBER

Kalawantis: Mr. Myers, you said that you served on the LFA Executive Committee. Are members of the Executive Committee appointed or elected?

Mr. Brucien Myers: Members of the Executive Committee are elected for a two-year term. I was elected and then re-elected consecutively for three terms.

Kalawantis: So what time period was your service?

Mr. Brucien Myers: I served on the Executive Committee for a period of six years, from 1996 to 2001. Then I left and traveled to the United States of America.

Kalawantis:. I know we are talking football right now, as it relates to the Lone Star and the Liberia Football Association, what about all other sports activities? Does the LFA play any role in other sports, like basketball, kickball, softball, to name but a few.

Mr. Brucien Myers: No, the LFA has no role to play in any other sports. It is limited only to Football. The other sports you are referring to are separate organizations.

In addition to the information we received from Mr. Myers, further research by our team has revealed more insight about the Executive Committee.

"Administratively, the LFA is headed by a president (obviously) who is elected along with 12 other officials for a period of four years. The elected body is known as the Executive Committee, which is the highest decision making body in the absence of the Congress." This additional information we obtained from the website of the LFA.

We wanted to get more details about the 'Congress', or the composition and duties thereof. Unfortunately, we did not succeed in doing so.

During Mr. Myers' time on the Executive Committee, the term of office for elected officials might have been two years, but that number has doubled. Members are now elected for a period four years, according to the LFA website.

It goes without saying, 'time changes so very rapidly, as society progresses tremendously.'

LONE STAR PHOTO GALLERY

Jaytoe Anthony Tukan

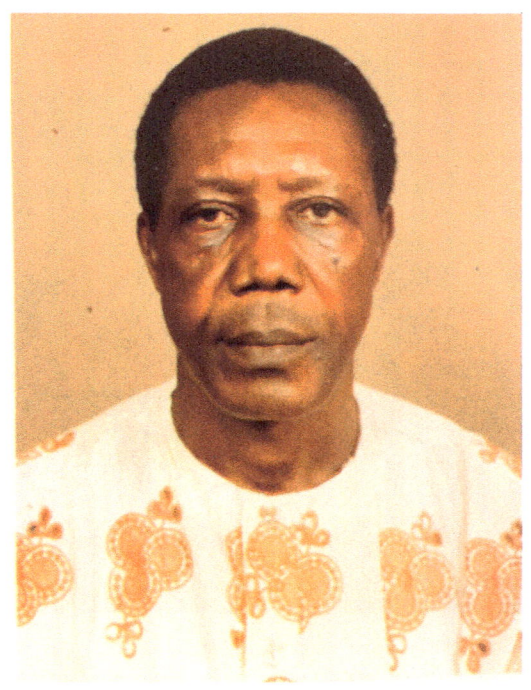

'Monkey' Brown

Author poses with Babe Ray

Author poses with Solo

Author poses with Rock of Gibraltar

Jaytoe Anthony Tukan

'Ansu'

George Opong Weah

Jaytoe Anthony Tukan

'Lucky Shango'

The Lone Star

Jaytoe Anthony Tukan

Liberian National Anthem

All hail, Liberia, hail! (All hail!)
All hail, Liberia, hail! (All hail!)
This glorious land of liberty
Shall long be ours.

Though new her name,
Green be her fame,
And mighty be her powers,
And mighty be her powers,

In joy and gladness
With our hearts united,
We'll shout the freedom
Of a race benighted,

Long live Liberia, happy land!
A home of glorious liberty, By God's command!
A home of glorious liberty, By God's command!

Jaytoe Anthony Tukan   179

II

All hail, Liberia, hail! (All hail!)
All hail, Liberia, hail! (All hail!)
In union strong success is sure
We cannot fail!

With God above
Our rights to prove
We will o'er all prevail,
We will o'er all prevail,

With heart and hand
Our country's cause defending
We'll meet the foe
With valor unpretending.

Long live Liberia, happy land!
A home of glorious liberty, By God's command!
A home of glorious liberty, By God's command!

Lyrics: Daniel B. Warner;Music: Olmstead Luca

Jaytoe Anthony Tukan

LIBERIA

This Sweet Land of Liberty
Long live Liberia, Long live Liberia!

Jaytoe Anthony Tukan

Made in the USA
Columbia, SC
02 August 2023

21014765R00104